D1826608

RALLY
PAST, PRESENT & FUTURE

RALLY
PAST, PRESENT & FUTURE

By Graham Ashby

Rally: Past, Present & Future
Published by
Graham & Wanda Ashby Ministries
with Castle Publishing Ltd
New Zealand

© 2022 Graham Ashby

ISBN 978-0-473-61756-1 (Softcover)
ISBN 978-0-473-61757-8 (ePUB)
ISBN 978-0-473-61758-5 (Kindle)

Editing: Geoff Vause

Production & Typesetting:
Andrew Killick
Castle Publishing Services
www.castlepublishing.co.nz

Cover Design:
Paul Smith & Graham Ashby

Cover images, left to right from top: Southland and Otago contingent travelling to 1982 Rally Arura; 1930-1935 Boys' Club established by Leo Clarke as the forerunner to Every Boy's Rally; Leo Clarke; Les Harris; staff at Clarkes Cycle Works; Bill Pratney advertising Clarkes Leader Racing Cycles; Kawarau jet boat sold by the Melhop brothers to establish a campsite to support Rally work; Short Solent Flying Boat that carried Leo Clarke to Sydney to promote Rally work in 1950; Rallies marching, 1982 Rally Arura, Tōtara Springs, Matamata.

Dedicated to the men and women
who gave their love, time and energy to the
Rally movement over the last 77 years.
They took their local dreams to heaven and
the Lord responded by growing an
international movement among them.
They prayed, breathed and spoke
the words of God to boys and girls.
Thousands are in heaven today because of them.
We salute their faith.
Some names we remember, other names
may be forgotten, but their
legacy of faith and purpose lives on.
Heaven will not forget them.

Then those who feared the LORD talked with each other,
and the LORD listened and heard.
A scroll of remembrance was written in His presence
concerning those who feared the LORD
and honoured His name.
Malachi 3:16

CONTENTS

PREFACE

This booklet expresses my deep gratitude to the New Zealand Every Boy's and Every Girl's Rally movement. Under God's hand this home-grown movement became a dynamic international organisation and over the years has helped countless lives. I was one of them. Among the early Rally leaders in Auckland, Laurie and Ernie Mayes brought the light of hope into my dark life. The truth they taught and modelled won my suspicious heart and helped set my life on a positive trajectory I could never have expected.

When men and women believe with all their hearts, souls and minds that children need the hope coming from knowing Jesus Christ, the Lord Himself will bless their efforts. The love and commitment of Rally leaders around the world contributed to better homes, happier communities, stronger churches and improved societies.

It is my prayer that this brief look at Rally's past, present and future will encourage and motivate its existing and future leaders to stay true to the intent of the Rally aims. They remain the guardians of our frontline outreach to the children of the world. May all who read this become supporters, friends, helpers and prayer partners of this anointed movement.

Acknowledgements: I am grateful to Robert Park for collecting valuable data from the Open Brethren heritage churches. It is a rich and generous source of information that could have so easily been lost.

Bruce Clarke (Leo Clarke's nephew), Murray Harris (son of Les Harris), David Burt, Catherine Birch, Fred King, John Massam, Norman Lind and Stuart Bay have contributed their combined experiences to help bring together the necessary information needed for this book. I am grateful for the guidance, love and support they gave to make this publication happen. May it all help the next generation.

Graham Ashby

1

HISTORY

Nineteen forty-four was a year of fear, turmoil, tragedy and sadness.

The world was at war for the second time in history. Millions of soldiers had died on the battlefields of Europe and millions of suffering civilians died or were displaced as powerful countries wrestled for political and territorial domination. The nations surrounding the Pacific Rim anxiously held their breath at the unrest and global hostility.

World newspaper headlines in 1944 included:

- Russian troops cross into Poland
- Japan attacks Burma
- Jews arrive at Auschwitz
- Japan attacks China
- Hitler orders Paris to be destroyed

New Zealand may have been far from the conflicts, but many of our men and women had been engaged in the fight for freedom.

The nation was still mourning 16,697 soldiers killed in WW1, with 11,625 of our own already dead on the battlefields of WW2. We still had 195,000 men and 10,000 women serving overseas. Submarines had been spotted surveying our coastlines.

New Zealand newspaper headlines of 1944 included:

- New Zealand forces capture Castle Hill at Cassino
- CORSO formed
- Kiwi pilot's sacrifice saves French village
- Meat rationing introduced
- Refugees from Europe arrive in New Zealand
- 200 American deserters at large in New Zealand

The 1944 War Budget was £152.9 million, and the Social Security bill was £17.7 million.

The Labour Government's Social Security Act of 1938 helped many homes stabilise their finances. This was particularly helpful for the almost 48,500 widowers and widows who were sole bread-winners, many of whom had been left without family members due to war.[1] Single mothers were initially denied the benefit and had to negotiate much red-tape to receive the state allowance.

Although the mood of the nation in 1944 was subdued and skittish, an idea to teach and encourage the boys of Auckland was established, not by politicians or soldiers, but by a bike merchant and a gifted educator.

Leo Berkely Clarke

Leo Clarke (pictured) had owned and operated Clarkes Cycle Works for several years and became one of the North Island's most important race frame builders.

He established his first shop in Newmarket, Auckland, in the mid-1920s. Later two more shops were opened, both in Auckland city, where he sold a brand known as Leaders.

Apart from those using their bikes for jobs such as newspaper deliveries, amongst Leo's regular clients were young men who competed in cycle races. He began to sponsor riders on his brand and quickly established a reputation for quality race bikes ridden by some of New Zealand's best professional riders.

Among them was Bill Pratney, known as the 'Iron Man' of cycling. Bill Pratney was raised in an orphanage after his mother and grandmother died.

As a teenager, Bill won local running and cycling races and decided to concentrate on cycling. In 1930 he was involved in a head-on bicycle crash with other racing cyclists and after being in a coma for three days doctors said he would never cycle again.

Three months after the accident he was back on his bike and in 1934 he won the fastest time in the 120-mile Round-the-Mountain Race at Taranaki.

His road racing career peaked in 1937 when he beat the great Harry Watson in the New Zealand 100-mile Road Championships.[2]

Leo Clarke had taken Bill under his wing, and with this father-like figure guiding and encouraging, Bill went on to become New Zealand's greatest Māori cyclist.[3]

As early as 1931, Leo Clarke had been holding informal classes to teach boys how to fix and maintain their bikes. As interest grew, he rented a tin shed in Newmarket (where the Olympic Pool now stands), and it didn't take long before 100 boys were gathering every week to learn practical skills. Bigger premises were soon found to accommodate the interest.

Leo was a prominent member of Ngaire Avenue Gospel Hall,[4] which at that time was one of the leading Assemblies[5] in Auckland.

Ngaire Avenue church was influential in starting Assemblies in Onehunga (Inkerman St), Ellerslie, Tāmaki, Sylvia Park and Māngere.

Before WW2 started, Leo was involved in a ministry to overseas sailors visiting the Port of Auckland. On Sunday afternoons, Leo, his brother Ernest and others, would drive to the wharves and invite sailors to Ngaire Avenue Gospel Hall for a meal.

They met in a room built on the back of the church and many knew it as 'the sailor's room'. A good meal was given and a Gospel message was shared. During the war the port area was locked off and the ministry ceased.

Every Sunday morning the Clarke family picked up four children from the Morris family to bring them to Sunday School. One of the children, Ray, became a missionary and first went to the Congo in Africa, before relocating to Winslow in Arizona. Ray and his wife established a successful youth work known as Boy's Rally among the Navajo and Hopi Indians.[6]

Leo gave significant practical support to the Christmas Camp at Willow Park, Auckland Bible Classes (ABC) with their annual picnics and quarterly rallies, Missionary Camps, Winter-house Party, Easter Camps and Conferences.

The annual ABC Picnic saw upward of 2,000 families, children and young people pack the ferries to Motuihe, and later Waiheke Island. The quarterly Christian Youth Crusade (CYC) rallies growing from the ABC, packed the YMCA Stadium, helping many young people come to faith.

Leo was also evangelically active with other Auckland Assembly Members, including Robert Laidlaw. All supported the Bible Training Institute (now Laidlaw College), Postal Sunday School Mission (PSSM), Scripture Gift Mission, Christian Businessmen's Association, YMCA, Youth For Christ (YFC), the Willow Park Camp and the Ngāruawāhia Easter Camp.

Leo worked with many other lay leaders and clergy across all denominations to help organise the Billy Graham Crusades of 1959 and 1969.

But life had not been easy for Leo. Born in 1905, he was nine years old when WW1 broke out. Auckland had gas street lamps and there was no domestic electricity supplied to homes.

In 1913 Leo's sister Betty was born and six years later the youngest brother Ernest joined the family.

Aged 13, Leo and his siblings survived the 1918 Influenza Pandemic which in two months claimed the lives of 9,000 New Zealanders. No other event had killed so many New Zealanders in such a short time.[7]

The Clarke family were shattered when Leo's father walked out on them all. Leo stepped up and helped the family through this crisis. He became the father figure in the home, carrying his mother, sister and brother through that difficult period.

Post-war, in 1921-22, New Zealand experienced a sharp recession. Another downturn shocked the economy in 1926, and during those years Leo Clarke opened Clarkes Cycle Works.

In 1928, aged 23, Leo married Winifred Florence Scott.

By 1931, New Zealand was in the Great Depression. Almost every family struggled economically. Seventy-thousand working adults were unemployed.

There were no social benefits. Making ends meet was a daily struggle, and unable to have children of their own, Leo and Winifred adopted two boys, Peter and Stanley.

Despite the demanding times Leo managed to expand his trade. He added lawnmover sales and services to the business, and in the late 60s combined home appliances. Televisions were a specialty.

During those early business years, Leo was motivated to help other broken families and offered encouragement to boys from troubled homes.

Leo's business mind gave him the idea of offering hire purchase agreements. This meant poorer boys could take immediate possession of a bicycle and pay it off over weekly instalments.

One dubious character took up the same offer and paid Clarkes Cycles the minimum of 3 shillings and 9 pence to ride the bicycle out the door.

He promptly took the new bicycle to another dealer and sold it 'brand new' for £2. It was a great profiteering venture until the police got involved and arrested him for stealing.

Percy Lewis Ward was sentenced to three months imprisonment but scathingly, Police Chief-Detective Hamond said, 'I have no sympathy for a firm that allowed such men as Ward to walk away with an expensive bicycle for 3s/9p.'

Leo Clarke was a Christian and recognised boys needed more than just fix-it skills to set them up as better men.

He believed more than anything else, they needed hope. Hope for the day and hope for the future. He prayed about the direction and purpose of developing a programme to make a significant spiritual and practical impact in boy's lives.

In 1944 Leo led the drive to start Every Boy's Rally.

While working hard to maintain his business and multiply the Rally initiative, Winifred became ill with cancer. In 1953 the illness took his wife from him.

Leo Clarke was a successful businessman and could have applied his greater energies and skills to growing his business ventures. The demand for bicycles, mowers and home appliances was strong.

With his work ethic and purposeful spirit, he could have developed the business much further. He chose to be more intentional with helping boys' hearts. Building character and offering the free gift of eternal life was more important than monetary gain.

Leo married Mary Walker in 1954 and she became a great encouragement to him in advancing the Rally work.

In 1955, aged 50, he retired and sold his business to a Baptist gentleman, Enoch Bond, who built it into Bond & Bond, the successful home appliance business.

Leo died aged 73, while mowing his lawns on May 18, 1978. His will ensured Mary and his sons were catered for. He left several bequeaths to his favourite organisations, and heading the list was a $1,000 gift to the Auckland Every Boy's and Every Girl's Rallies.

Back in 1944, supporting Leo's idea of starting the Every Boy's Rally had been his good friend Les Harris.

Leslie Arthur Harris

Les Harris (pictured) was born October 10, 1895, one year before the first motor car was built in New Zealand and seven years before Timaru's Richard Pearse's pioneering first flight in his homemade aircraft.

Les Harris was an outstanding man. Although nothing is known of his early years, when WW1 broke out, at age 20 Les enlisted as a Gunner with the New Zealand Army.

On the Western Front he fought with the Allied Troops at Passchendaele, Flanders, Belgium. The misery of Passchendaele was compounded with New Zealand suffering more than 18,000 casualties – including 5,000 deaths.[8]

Passchendaele is known as New Zealand's 'blackest day', our greatest horror of the Great War. As an artillery gunner, Les Harris was among the turmoil.

Wounded in battle, Les faced a lengthy recovery period in England before he was returned home.

His War Records show the gunshot wound to his head gave him persistent headaches, and the shrapnel scar on his leg was a visible reminder of all he had endured.

He was declared unfit for war and discharged from duty on July 15, 1918. He served 219 days in New Zealand, and one year, 164 days overseas. Les was awarded the Victory Medal for his services to Queen and country. Four of his day-by-day diaries are now in the Auckland War Memorial Museum.

After his discharge, Les returned to his career as a school-teacher. This led to him holding the position of Headmaster at Kaikohe, Birkenhead, Ruawai and Orakei Schools. Recognised as a leader, Orakei Primary was the largest primary school in the country at the time of his appointment.

'He was fair and his wise judgment and counsel were notable qualities which benefited many. He was frank and always expressed a clear opinion when required.'[9]

Post-war, Les was meeting with the Open Brethren at the Ngaire Avenue Gospel Hall, possibly because during the early Rally days the Harris family lived next door to the Clarke family in Greenlane.

Les married Jessie Fairgray in 1919 and together they raised five lads, Bruce, Evan, Don, Robin and Murray.

Except for Robin, who became an accountant, all the boys chose teaching careers which led to academic positions around the world.

Jessie Harris died in 1971.

Of his parents, Murray wrote, 'We were encouraged in our schoolwork and sporting pursuits. Our parents taught us Christian truth and Christian morals, and themselves embodied a Christian lifestyle and worldview for us to follow.

'For fifty years my father served on the New Zealand Council of SIM (Sudan Interior Mission, as it was then called), for many of those years as chairman.'[10]

Later, Les married Helen Haughey.

The sharp intelligence and precise work Les was known for were harnessed to prepare the *Boys' Manual*, the *Rally Leaders' Handbook* and the devotional outlines used among the Rallies.[11]

Les Harris died September 11, 1984.

On a warm summer's evening, January 17, 1944, Leo Clarke and Les Harris met at the Howe Street Gospel Hall with 30 representatives from eight other Assemblies.

After opening in prayer their discussions centred on how they could effectively conduct a well-balanced programme of spiritual, mental and physical activities for boys. As the meeting progressed it became obvious there was a definite need for a work of this kind.

They formed a Christian youth movement to be known as Every Boy's Rally (EBR).

It would be a place where, every week, boys from across Auckland could come and be taught a variety of life skills, have fun and games, but more importantly to hear the Good News of Jesus Christ.

The boys would have a uniform and the programme would have its disciplines and achievement rewards acknowledged with badges. The aim of this new venture was set out in the *Rally Objective*:

- To build strong Christian character in children,
- to increase their knowledge and understanding,
- to help them physically,
- and to give good team confidence and co-operation.

The *Rally Motto* came directly from the Bible:

> *Honour all men, love the brotherhood,*
> *fear God, honour the king.*[12]

Closing in prayer, they placed this movement completely into God's hands. Learning about this new youth initiative, Robert Laidlaw, a friend to Clarke and Harris who owned and managed the Farmers Trading Company, offered to support them.

Starting Every Boy's Rally was not an original idea. The Open Brethren church that Clarke, Harris and Laidlaw were part of had seen successful work done among the military training camps in New Zealand.

Known as the Everyman's Huts, Christian men had been involved with soldiers in training at the various military venues. They entered these camps and gave soldiers reading material and conducted programmes where a sermon was always given.

These meetings were so popular the army permitted the construction of prefabricated huts to be placed in their compounds. These huts were manned by full-time Christian workers.

Some of these workers had previous involvement in the once prominent Bible Carriages and were experienced in sharing the Scriptures and leading people to faith.

Many despairing soldiers were helped and encouraged, and became Christians during those times. The success of the Everyman's Huts outreaches had stirred Leo Clarke into developing a similar work among the boys he was mentoring.

His deepest concern was for their spiritual well-being, which was to be complemented by the practical instructions on the nuts and bolts of life.

The challenge before these good men was real. The world was still at war and thousands of New Zealanders remained actively involved.

Families grieved as their men were lost at war and children would now be raised without a father's influence. At the same time, incomes were tight, fear prevailed and many lacked hope.

We do not know the exact discussion at the Howe Street church meeting in January of 1944, but what we do know:

They were unanimous in agreeing they could not be passive when the need was so great.

They would stand united in their efforts to reach the souls of Auckland boys.

Collectively, they would proclaim the Gospel through this movement.

Leo Clarke was a capable and respected businessman whose resilience and determination grew his business through a very difficult period in New Zealand's history.

Facing many financial and domestic challenges, he rose above them all and found the time to invest spiritual, moral and social truths into the lives of many others.

Les Harris, a battler, a survivor and an accomplished leader put the war behind him and believed the best way forward for the country was to educate the nation's children.

As a teacher and headmaster, he gave his expertise to using education as a way to teach the Gospel to the boys and girls of New Zealand.

In God's goodness, providentially, Leo and Les became neighbours.

As a team, Leo Clarke and Les Harris constructed a positive and consummate relationship, developing one of the most enduring youth outreach programmes of the New Zealand Open Brethren heritage churches. Another strong initiative was Christian camping ministries.

In 1944 New Zealand's children needed hope. What did a distinguished businessman with practical abilities and a returned soldier with remarkable teaching skills do?

They stepped out in faith.

2

HOPE

We can't be sure who originally penned the words 'Cometh the hour cometh the man.' They characterised Sir Winston Churchill and described the marvel that sometimes, when a hero is needed, one appears.

In the case of beginning the Every Boy's Rally (EBR) movement, 'Cometh the hour cometh the *men*.' Not just one, but two.

Like the prophets of old, Leo Clarke had a vision and became the leader of this God-honouring movement. Close behind was the scribe Les Harris. His administration and organisational skill-set enabled him to document the narrative and instruct the way ahead.

Between 1926 and 1936, New Zealand census data shows that the Open Brethren movement had grown by 5,000. There were many more who identified with this group but would never admit on a census they were aligned to a denomination. But the growth in numbers showed the outreach work of their Tent Meetings and the Everyman's Huts.

The many volunteers saw fruit for their labours. It was hoped the men who volunteered their time to EBR work would also reap a harvest of young lives for the Lord.

In the early 1900s the emphasis was on ministering to the more mature.[1] But work among children was a growing feature of the Open Brethren during those years. As early as 1914, the Open

Brethren church in Ashburton pioneered week-night children's activities.

In 1944 there were youth programmes in the form of Bible Classes for older teens. At the same time, many good Sunday Schools were running in Wellington, the Waikato, the Manawatū, Christchurch, Dunedin and Invercargill.

In addition to Sunday School, some clubs for boys and girls were running in Wellington and a few of the Auckland Open Brethren churches.

By 1944 attitudes had changed and people like Clarke and Harris could see reaching the children of a hurting nation was now a priority.

One of the strong commitments the Open Brethren heritage churches had was a genuine desire to bring the Good News of Jesus Christ to help heal a wounded country.

The obedience to 'Go and make disciples of all nations, baptising them in the name of the Father and of the Son and of the Holy Spirit' (Matthew 28:19) was their motivator.

Brethren were often seen preaching on the streets around the nation, conducting Tent Outreach meetings and were involved in the Every Man's Hut endeavours. The new EBR concept added another witness opportunity.

Growing the EBR weekly programme of practical everyday handyman skills, accompanied by games and physical activities to stimulate a boy's mind, heart, body and soul was quite the undertaking.

There We Found Brethren, by Dr Peter Lineham, shows that post-war there were no Open Brethren employed in cinemas, on racetracks, or in liquor and tobacco industries.[2]

Few worked in transport, including shipping and the railways. Even less worked in the sawmilling and mining industries. In contrast quite high numbers were shopkeepers, bankers and dealers of various kinds.

Of the 17,000 people who belonged to the Assemblies, only 173 were sheep farmers. It was in the dairying regions like the Manawatū, Nelson and the Waikato where more practical farmers were found – 572 of them.

Most of New Zealand's young men were offshore in 1944 fighting the war and apart from the lads working on farms, those who remained probably weren't that practical with their hands.

The men who began the EBR movement were older professional men. Leo Clarke, a practical man, was 39 years old when he started Every Boy's Rally and Les Harris, a meticulous man, was 48.

In 1944, Auckland was the largest and fastest growing city in New Zealand. Between the two World Wars twelve Assemblies were founded across the city. Those who held conservative views didn't involve themselves in this new work.

Undeterred, Clarke and Harris pressed on with their vision. This wasn't about them. It was a resolute commitment to help and encourage the boys of Auckland and other regions with the truth of the Gospel message.

In the weeks following the establishment of EBR, the signs of hope were encouraging.

Other Assemblies in the city showed their interest. Many agreed with reaching the boys of Auckland with the Gospel, but most needed training in how to establish their respective Rally and what to do at each programme.

Consequently, in 1944 Every Boy's Rally Camp was launched. The first combined camp was held at Eastern Beach at a cost of 3/6 pence per boy.

The same year, in the Wellington area, with the enthusiasm and vision of Jim Finn (who may have been at the initial January meeting in Auckland), Rally work started in the Hutt Valley at Moera.

A year after the EBR was established, there was a groundswell of interest from the ladies of the Auckland churches believing an Every Girl's Rally (EGR) would be beneficial.

Before 1944 many women were already involved in ministries that supported young girls and young women. There had been clubs organised for girls in the 1930s and their leaders were enthusiastic about developing a stronger, more formal organisation. Working beside the EBR development made perfect sense.

On March 12, 1945, a committee was formed with Lillian Laidlaw and Nettie Burt as leaders. A pattern began to emerge around the country: once an EBR started, an EGR soon followed.

Partnering with EBR turned out to be a significant development because having outstanding women leaders complemented and enhanced the new movement.

'Cometh the hour cometh the women.'

The energy and eagerness displayed by the early Rally leaders resulted in Rallies popping up in many rural and urban places. Rally work was embraced throughout the Open Brethren movement in New Zealand and it soon became the evangelical focal point. The inauguration of Rallies to reach the children of the day created a sincere solidarity among the Assemblies.

Official minutes from some of the early meetings show the EBR and EGR grew so fast and was in such great demand around the country their biggest problem was finding enough leaders.

During those early thriving years, Leo Clarke and Jack McCracken boarded the Short Solent Flying Boat (no passports required) for Sydney, Australia. It was a tedious eight-hour flight, but their purpose was to promote the EBR and EGR idea to the Open Brethren Assemblies there.

In 1950, Rallies started in New South Wales and Queensland. The same year Rallies were introduced in Suva, Fiji. In 1951, Rally work began in Victoria. The movement was becoming international.

Clarke's strategy was simple: find the key people in each country and explain to them the potential and importance of reaching boys and girls for Christ.

The founders of the Rally movement advanced in faith not knowing what they would see. Hoping their vision would become a reality they pressed on. Their confidence was in Christ, and they poured their lives, talents and dreams into the Rally mission.

In 1958, Leo Clarke went on holiday to Northern Ireland and talked about how the Rally work had become an effective outreach in many communities. Several interested Assembly leaders were invited to meet him and learn about the work.

The youth leaders who met at the Victoria Memorial Hall in May Street, Belfast, had been looking at the possibility of introducing a structured, uniformed organisation with a strong spiritual influence.

They wanted to share the message of Christ to boys and girls. On hearing of the Rally aims and expanding influence, they realised it was what they were looking for.[3]

A group met to discuss forming Rallies in Northern Ireland. Uniforms were chosen and an overall programme suitable for their members was organised.

In 1958, the first Northern Ireland Every Boy's Rally was started in Victoria Memorial Hall, Belfast. Every Girl's Rally started the following year. Soon other churches and assemblies decided to adopt the Rally movement.

As in New Zealand and Australia, the Rally work in Northern Ireland became the premier outreach work to the youth of that nation.

In Northern Ireland there was a special significance to their work. As the sectarian fighting increased among Catholic and Protestant groups, the uniformed and disciplined Rally work became a neutral and non-violent organisation for both denominations to send their boys and girls to.

At Rally they learnt to march (the Irish love their marching), had uniforms, were part of a disciplined group, would learn life skills and hear messages from the Bible.

This was accepted by Catholic and Protestant families and, even better, no guns were involved.

The Bible says, 'Faith is being sure of what we hope for and certain of what we do not see' (Hebrews 11:1).

Leo Clarke, Les Harris and the many men and women who believed in this work had stepped out in faith. They prayed, worked, gave of themselves and hoped the Lord would use their efforts to change boys and girls lives for the better.

Their vision was real, but none had envisaged it would go so far so quickly. Their prayers were answered and nationally what they hoped for came about because of their obedient faith.

Like the dynamic Old Testament friendship of Joshua and Caleb, Leo Clarke and Les Harris trusted the Lord, maintained their hope, and saw the Lord do many things beyond their expectations.

Leo and Les, with Mrs Laidlaw and Miss Burt, witnessed the beginning of the EBR and EGR and prayed God would use it to reach thousands of children around the world.

Their compliance and commitment to 'Go and make disciples' had grown an international movement.

3

GROWTH

As people in the Assemblies across New Zealand learned about the effectiveness of the Rally work, more Rallies began to expand through the country.

The main form of evangelism in the 1950s was open-air preaching, tent meetings and tract distribution, concentrated on adults. But the Rallies' contemporary objective to reach children was welcome and requests on how to start and conduct a Rally kept coming.

In 1946 the first Waikato/Bay of Plenty leaders' meeting was held. Mr Clarke and Mr Harris attended with thirteen Assemblies represented.

The minutes from that meeting say, 'it was a most inspiring gathering.' A District Committee was set up under M.C.G. Gauntlett and Secretary Isa Hughes.

On February 21, 1948, the first EGR Workers Retreat was held at Willow Park Camp. Rallies in Auckland were so big on the evening of July 13, 1949, a combined EBR and EGR was held at the Concert Chambers of the Auckland Town Hall.

In 1951 the first edition of the *Every Boy's and Every Girl's Rally Leaders Bulletin* was printed. Edited by Les Marsh, he wrote in his opening comments:

Six years of Rally life have slipped into the past. With them have gone many moments of great joy in achievements recorded for eternity. Souls of youth are rejoicing in salvation; lives of youth have been dedicated to the Master.

With the years, too, have gone many uneasy moments as mistakes have been revealed and written off as bitter experience.

In short, the Rally Movement has passed its first flush of birth and childhood and now looks to some steady all-round growth.

The past has not been easy; the future is going to be harder.

The editor's remarks showed establishing a national organisation was bigger than anyone could have imagined, and they had reaped a small harvest of young lives for the Lord.

Their faith, vision and commitment had been rewarded. Knowing they had successfully come through the teething problems, like faithful parents they pressed on to take Rally in the adolescent stage.

Now it was onward and upward.

The explosion of interest in the early 1950s from many of the New Zealand Assemblies resulted in Rallies being established in numerous locations:

Northland: Kaikohe, Hikurangi, Kamo, Whangārei, Onerahi.

Auckland: Takapuna, Birkenhead, Bayswater, St Heliers, Newton (Howe Street), Mount Albert, Balmoral (Wiremu Street), Eden, Epsom (Ngaire Avenue), Ellerslie, Glen Innes, Onehunga, Papatoetoe, Mount Roskill, Tāmaki, Te Papapa, Waikōwhai.

Hauraki/Coromandel: Waiuku, Thames, Whitianga.

Waikato/Bay of Plenty: Hamilton, Cambridge, Frankton, Rotorua, Morrinsville, Springdale and Waihi, Katikati, Manawarū, Tahuna, Tauwhare, Mt Maunganui, Mangateparu, Orini, Paeroa, Putāruru, Tauranga, Tokoroa, Te Puke, Te Awamutu, Tauhei, Te Aroha, Taupiri, Waharoa, Matamata, Waerenga.

King Country: Te Kuiti, Taumarunui, Ōhura, Ōwhango.

Manawatū/Whanganui: Marton, Bulls, Feilding, Foxton, Palmerston North, Rongotea, Bunnythorpe, Ashhurst, Dannevirke, Woodville, Pahiatua, Whanganui.

Taranaki: New Plymouth.

Poverty Bay: Gisborne.

Hawkes Bay: Napier, Hastings.

Wairarapa: Masterton, Carterton, Greytown.

Horowhenua: Levin, Ōtaki, Poroutawhao.

Hutt Valley: Moera, Heretaunga, Belmont, Naenae, Epuni, Petone.

Wellington: Tory Street, Vivian Street, Johnsonville, Khandallah, Newtown, Taitā.

Nelson: Nelson, Stoke, Hope.

Canterbury: St Albans (Rutland Street), Bryndwr, Riccarton,

Waltham, Quinn's Road, Darfield, Glentunnel, Ashburton, Hororata.

Otago: Oamaru, Duntroon, Kaikorai, South Dunedin.

Southland: Invercargill (Don Street).

In six busy years, there were at least 100 Rallies fully functioning throughout New Zealand.

Internationally, the Rally movement also continued to grow. Following on from the Rallies started in New South Wales, Queensland and Fiji in 1950, Rally work began in Victoria in 1951, and in 1952 two Every Girl's Rallies started in India. The Rally movement started in Samoa in 1955.

In 1958 when the Rally work began in Northern Ireland, the Open Brethren churches there were strong in numbers and committed to proclaiming the Gospel.

As news spread about this new idea to communicate the Gospel to boys and girls, the progressive assemblies decided to adopt the Rally movement. Among them were the Crescent Church in Belfast which, as well as its own Rally, formed three other Rallies in the estates of Braniel, Seaview and Rathcoole.

Bethany Gospel Hall in Finaghy, Brooklands Gospel Hall in Dundonald, Woodford Gospel Hall in Armagh, Dunclug Gospel Hall in Ballymena and the Scrabo Gospel Hall in Newtownards all established long-standing Rallies.

Although there were a good number of Brethren Assemblies in Northern Ireland in 1958, some of the more conservative churches frowned upon the perceived revelry their fellow Christians were undertaking to entertain the youth. Sadly, these churches distanced themselves from the Rally work.

Twenty-three years later in 1981, the Limerick Rally at Enniskillen in Northern Ireland was formed. At their peak, there were hundreds of leaders and Irish boys and girls involved in the Northern and Southern Ireland Rallies, many of whom came to faith in Christ their Saviour. At the time of writing, Rallies still meet in five venues across Northern Ireland.[1]

As the influence of Rally spread around the world it quickly became apparent the organisation needed a more consolidated leadership to help with policies, programmes and promotion.

The first coordinated idea was the development of Rally Supplies. Right from the start, Rally Supplies became the one connection point for all Rallies who needed badges, uniforms, magazines, banners, cookbooks and information.

Initially, the Rally Supplies base was in Auckland, but in the late 1990s moved to the Gospel Publishing House building in Palmerston North.

Managed by various volunteering women, it has been the vital provider of all things Rally for more than seventy years. Now situated in the Waikato, Ruth Turner continues this essential service.

Palmerston North hosted a national conference in 1961, where the decision was made to form a New Zealand Rally Council. Harold Melhop from Invercargill was invited to be the chairman and Jim Coppin the secretary. The National Council was important not only to advise the growing movement, but also to negotiate with government over funding. At the time, all uniformed youth groups received an annual Government payment per person. This helped fund Rally Council programmes and resources.

Harold Melhop and his brother Alan were successful businessmen who owned an Invercargill engineering business. In 1958 they were the first men to navigate below the Kawarau Falls Dam in their Hamilton jet boat.

They soon found holidaymakers would line up for rides on the thrilling new boat. Starting at only five shillings a ride, they began the world's first commercial jet boating operation.

They were also enthusiastic about sharing their Christian faith with the boys and girls of Southland and with others formed a trust to obtain land and build a Christian Camp.

The brothers sold their tourist business to build the dream. Land was gazetted by the government of the day for youth camp work and in 1959 the Melhops led the trust to build on the site now known as Lakeland Park Christian Camp & Convention Centre.

For generations the camp was the perfect complement to the Rally work with boys and girls from Southland to Otago enjoying many memorable times there.

Harold's skills and zeal made him the perfect chairman to advance the vision and direction of the EBR and EGR. Together, Harold and Alan gave 100 years of service to the Rally work.

What happened in Queenstown was repeated elsewhere. In 1962, Hikurangi Island in Lake Whakamaru was seen as a good place to establish a camp.

Hikurangi Island was established by the damming of the Waikato River which formed Lake Whakamaru. The trust board at the time was given a 99-year lease with an annual peppercorn rent.

Thomas (Tom) Lind developed the site. Tom had worked on the Manawatū/Taranaki Bible Carriage. He went to Mangakino in about 1956 to plant a church through Rally work and Bible in Schools. Lake Whakamaru camp became known as 'Tom Lind's Island'.

In 1963, the Auckland EBR bought a section at Moirs Point, Mangawhai, for a camp.

Meanwhile, the Willow Park Camp in Eastern Beach, Auckland, was used by the EBR and EGR annually during the initial years and still is. Camping became a great partner to the Rally work.

Another partner was the printing press (no photocopiers then). Les Harris had produced marvellous material to guide Rally leaders and children.

In 1953 Les Marsh and his family moved to Feilding[2] where he managed the Gospel Publishing House in Palmerston North. The publications and supplies followed his move.

Les co-edited the magazines with Fred Swallow in Auckland. Boys' and girls' publications were produced with Isa Hughes and Betty McConnell editing the Girl's magazines and Girl's Badge Manuals.

All these publications later became coeducational. So much was being produced that, in 1959, printers H.L. Thatcher & Sons Bookshop, who owned Auckland Bible House, took over the supply of Rally materials. They were later bought out by Gospel Publishing House (GPH).

There had been attempts to produce magazines that would be informative and interesting, such as the *Rally Ho* and *Rally News*. But in 1961, Volume 1 of the *Rally Standard* was printed for all Rally boys and girls, and superseded the previous publications.

The editor, Les Marsh, was known as 'Skipper' and children were encouraged to write and ask any question they were seeking an answer for.

This first edition of *Rally Standard* revealed the growth and reach the Rally movement had made over the preceding 17 years:

Prior to our movement being known as The Every Boy's

Rally, a few groups had been meeting for games, hobbies and outings in Auckland and other centres, but it was not until 1944 that we used our present name and were organised as a combined body.

Since then, our growth has been remarkable from several groups in Auckland to 150 Junior, Intermediate and Senior Rallies in towns and cities from Kaitaia to Invercargill.

The strength of the Rallies in New Zealand is 11,000 boys and girls, plus 1,000 Leaders and Assistant Leaders. The movement has also been established in Australia, Samoa, Fiji, Northern Ireland, and now in Arizona, USA.[3]

It also recorded that,

At their annual display, four Glen Innes Rallies (Auckland) combined to present the girls singing Māori action songs and figure marching.

This culminated in the forming of the letters E.B.R. and E.G.R. The boys played energetic games and gave a splendid display of gymnastics on the junior jumping jack. Robert Muldoon, M.P. [New Zealand Prime Minister from 1975 to 1984], spoke on the value of Rally work to the large number of parents and friends present. The evening concluded with a devotional talk by Auckland Liaison Officer Mr E.P. Clarke.[4]

Another notable piece of information was in an article '50 Years of Rally in the Wellington District', by Catherine Birch:

In October 1945 the Tory St EBR challenged the Newtown Boys to a game of soccer. Ian Johnstone was the referee and Newtown EBR won by 4 goals to 0. A penalty goal was kicked by Paul Reeves.[5]

Paul Reeves went on to train and be ordained as an Anglican clergyman, then Bishop. He served as Archbishop and Primate of New Zealand from 1980 to 1985 and became the 15th Governor-General of New Zealand, and first governor-general of Māori descent, from 20 November 1985 to 20 November 1990.

He was knighted and became The Hon and the Rt Rev Sir Paul Reeves, GCMG, GCVO, QSO. He also served as the third Chancellor of Auckland University of Technology, from 2005 until his death.[6]

It is encouraging to think that Newton EBR leaders either sowed or watered the spiritual seeds in young Paul Reeves' life.

Another milestone with print came when the Rally Council of New Zealand partnered with the New Zealand Bible Society and produced the unique *Rally Bible* for Rally members. Released in 2016, 5,000 copies were printed and distributed. A second edition was ordered in 2021.

Globally, the Rallies continued to flourish:

- 1960, Rallies started in Kasaji, Zaire, Africa.
- 1961, Rallies began in Winslow, Arizona, USA.
- 1964, first EGR started in Chester, England.
- 1965, Rally began at Sakeji Mission School, Zambia.
- 1967, Rally commenced at Anguganak, Papua New Guinea.
- 1978, Rally started in the Virgin Islands.

Meanwhile in New Zealand, by 1966 there were 332 rallies, with 11,545 children on the rolls.

Twenty years after the first Rally was established, New Zealand was a significantly different place.

Kiwis had a growing confidence that all was well, and their best years were ahead of them. The positive mood was in absolute contrast to the sadness and anxiety evident two decades earlier. Now, the economy and society were upbeat.

The prevailing feeling was focused on gratification and materialism. Historians record rugby, racing and beer were synonymous with defining the culture of the 1960s. The economy had slowed with the price of wool dropping, but the demand for our meat created a boom resulting in many from rural communities pouring into cities and towns to the freezing works.

Jobs were available and the money was excellent. The passive rural drift into cities in the 1960s had turned into a wave of urbanisation as people came to live in the big cities.

Many were apparently experiencing good times. The average income was £50 per week (equivalent to $991 today).[7]

Between the mid-1940s and the early 1970s, women averaged four births per family. In 1961, 65,476 babies were born into a population of 2.4 million.

New Zealand was a baby paradise. Wainuiomata in Lower Hutt was known as 'Nappy Valley'. More schools had to be built to educate the baby-boomer population.

But as is so often the case in society when pleasure becomes the predominant pursuit, its most innocent are neglected. All was not rosy in Aotearoa, the 'land of the long-white cloud'. There were areas in New Zealand where being a kid was quite the challenge. The real problem was adult dysfunction.

In places like Ōtara, South Auckland, many children had to navigate the horrors of alcohol abuse, substance abuse, family violence, sexual abuse, child abuse, gambling, gangs and poverty.

The adult indulgences created a difficult and treacherous path for their children. For a society that had so much going for it economically, behind closed doors, mental, social and emotional damage was happening to our most vulnerable.

It's troubling to know that, on the whole, the government ignored the cries for help coming from these urban ghettos.

As one who lived in Ōtara during those years, it was notable to me the good work of Scouts and Boy's Brigade were absent in the hot spot of South Auckland.

But all was not lost. By this stage, the Rally movement was growing in strength, confidence and in numbers. Boldly they ventured into the worst suburbs in New Zealand to offer Every Boy's and Every Girl's Rallies to all who would come.

Knowing a change of heart can change a life, these brave and humble leaders volunteered their time to reach into the dark streets of New Zealand with the message of light.

They modelled joy, fun and hope. They believed the message that 'God loves you' could help children find a purpose to their lives.

The early leaders knew that giving hurting children the example of positivity and fun while teaching the love of God would be the best way to help them overcome their environments.

Rally nights were not just about games, hobbies and food. The Rally leaders were intentional about speaking to all children about God's love for them to give them hope for the future.

This message was never compromised, and I believe their commitment to delivering the life changing message of Jesus was the reason the Lord expanded and blessed this movement.

Of course, there were challenges. I know of one incident that almost had serious consequences for the movement.

A boy from a South Auckland Rally was caught dragging his metal-plated shoes behind the back of a Rally van on the Auckland motorway. An angry policeman was not amused, fined the Rally Leader and took the matter to his superiors.

The Auckland Police Department called a special meeting which Mr Clarke and Mr Harris attended to explain the importance of the Rally work. The police were adamant the work should stop because of the unsafe way children were being transported.

Whatever Clarke and Harris said that day persuaded the police to allow the work to continue, albeit with extra precautionary measures.

I know the story because I was that boy!

Years later as I retold the story in the Papatoetoe Gospel Hall, an older lady rapidly approached me waving her finger under my nose.

Sternly, she said, 'So you're the boy, so you're the boy.' She went on to explain the entire Rally movement was worried the outreach work was about to cease because of the foolish actions of one boy.

Special prayer meetings were called around the country and pleas for understanding and sympathy were sent to police officials.

I could never have known my stupid behaviour came so close to ending an international movement. I write this brief history in penance.

The early Rally leaders gave audacious energy to grow the future movement.

All of them volunteered copious amounts of intensity and resources during their leadership years. It is a privilege to acknowledge names like Mary Clarke and Jessie Harris, the faithful wives who endorsed and affirmed their ardent husbands.

Without their support, patience and devoted encouragement the Rally movement could easily have faltered.

Mr and Mrs Jeffers, who designed the badge and motto book, are among the many names heaven knows about. Their steadfast and unswerving commitment to the Rally movement helped turn an amateur beginning into a proficient organisation embraced around the world.

I remain in awe of their enthusiastic momentum that grew into a global movement, all done on shoe-string budgets and with no personal compensation.

Since its inception in 1944 the Rally movement maintained a real and healthy momentum. Its reach went global and by the late 1970s, hundreds of leaders and thousands of children were involved in this thriving organisation.

I suggest the phenomenal growth distinctly affirmed three vital lessons.

Firstly, the Rally movement had the Lord's fingerprints all over it. He blessed every effort and enabled it to grow at a substantial rate. The full commitment and sincere Gospel focus of every leader was honoured by God.

Secondly, despite their autonomy, the Open Brethren Assemblies were connected. This was a low-tech era and communications were by word-of-mouth, telephone or letters.

The news was out, reaching youth would not only grow the Kingdom of heaven; Rally could enrich and grow churches.

The triumphs of the Rally work meant more Assemblies added youth halls to their facilities. If an existing hall had no scope to expand, buildings were sold and bigger premises found to cater for the young people coming to the church.

Rallies enhanced the unity of the Open Brethren heritage churches.

Thirdly, the Rally movement was truly a 'for such a time as this' organisation. Post-war, as many countries endeavoured to cater for fatherless children by supporting grieving families and attempting to rebuild hope into their communities – the Lord used the EBR and EGR to bring the love of God and the peace of the Saviour into many lives.

As the evidence of exponential growth reveals, that love, that kindness, that peace were embraced, and changed countless lives for the better.

During those wonderful and exhilarating days of growth, there was a time when the end of year celebrations for the Auckland Rallies were so well attended that the Auckland Town Hall had to be hired to accommodate the large numbers. Similarly, in 1975 when Australia accomplished 25 years of Rally work, the occasion was celebrated with a gathering in the concert hall of the Sydney Opera House. Leo Clark spoke to the substantial crowd, as did the New South Wales Minister of Recreation and Sport, and other notable dignitaries.

Would this momentum continue to grow, plateau or slow?[8]

4

ARURAS

Since the inception of the Rally work in 1944, the value of camps has been recognised as a strategic partner to enhance the lives of boys and girls.

As Rallies grew around the country, conducting an annual camp was often a highlight for Rally members. Going camping together was a positive opportunity to grow relationships, strengthen friendships and to have an adventure together.

It was also a rich time of learning as outdoor skills progressed to new levels and more time could be spent in explaining the Gospel message.

The good partnership between Rallies and camps had mutual benefits. As the Rallies thrived, the need for bigger camps increased. Camps expanded and new sites were developed to help connect more boys and girls with camping experiences. It was a win-win situation.

In his challenging and timely book *One Million Children* author Tony Collis says, 'It is believed that a one-week camp is equivalent in impact to two and a half years of Sunday School.'[1]

If that's the case, a week's camp is comparable to over one year of Rally programmes. Little wonder the Rally movement embraced the vitality and importance of conducting annual camps.

By 1970 the Rally movement was firmly established in a variety of countries around the world. In the mid-seventies there was growing enthusiasm for an International Camp to bring the nations together in one place.

The idea of the Aruras was born in that eagerness from leaders in New Zealand and overseas.

Arura is an Australian Aboriginal word meaning 'gathering at camp'. The term was adopted in 1978 at the first Arura hosted in Canberra, Australia. It was a week-long camp for Rally members from around the world to gather, meet and enjoy spiritual, physical, social and educational development.

Chairman of the New Zealand Rally Council, Harold Melhop, designed the International Arura flag flown for the first time at the Canberra Arura.

The event was a huge success with Rally members attending from almost every country Rallies were established.

After the elation of the Canberra Arura, it was agreed each Rally nation could host another of these significant events biannually. Eighteen International Aruras took place over a period of 37 years. Six were held in Australia, six in New Zealand and six were hosted in Northern Ireland.

The Aruras were all amazing in their own unique ways as leaders and Rally members experienced the wonderful cultures of the host nations.

The Lord did a mighty work during those special Aruras. The time together at each Arura bonded the movement in an astonishing way as lives were changed, equipped and encouraged to go on.

The founding fathers would have been thrilled with the developments.

The biggest Arura ever held was at Tōtara Springs Christian Centre, Matamata, Waikato, in 1982.

Almost 1,500 people gathered from Australia, India, Japan, Fiji, Zambia, Virgin Islands, England, Northern Ireland and all corners of New Zealand.

A large permanent sporting auditorium completed on site and on time for the Arura was a huge asset for the sporting requirements of such an event. It was a huge effort by all involved.

The day before the Arura was to start, a deluge of rain and an unprecedented hailstorm almost wrecked the plans as the campsite was turned into a series of frozen lakes. Undeterred, an army of volunteers erected temporary buildings, tents for accommodation, marquees, showers, toilets, tables, shops, offices, desks, telephone booths and flood lights. Places were organised for managers, speakers, counsellors, first-aid officers, shops and hobby areas.

The workers established a full public address system to the marquees, assembly areas, main concourse, swimming pool and main stage for the opening ceremony.

Eight devotion areas had to be set up, each equipped with power, piano, lights, screens and amplifiers. It took 40 cooks led by Daniel Arbuckle and a team of caterers to feed and clean up for so many people three times a day.

The weather was fine and warm through the entire Arura with only one hour of rain over the whole eight days.

Rally co-founder Les Harris, aged 86, was at this Arura. Surrounded by the colourful flags of every nation represented, in a firm clear voice, he spoke at the opening ceremony.

He told everyone how grateful he was to God in allowing him to see the great sight before him. Umbrella overhead, he stood there, frail but imposing as he said: 'I declare this, the second International Arura, open.'[2]

Les Harris then had the privilege of seeing over a thousand leaders and campers, in full uniform, amidst a sea of banners and flags, enthusiastically march past the podium.

He said: 'This was the most outstanding event in the history of the Rally Movement.'[3]

The programming extended into hobbies, games of all varieties, team events, swimming, athletics, talent quests and hobby electives. The choice of BMX, go-carts, eeling, tramping, horse riding and tourist bus trips to Rotorua or Tauranga was available to all.

The concluding comments from Robert (Bob) Jackson, member of the Rally Council, captured the mood:

> The results of this Arura will remain with us for a long time. For some an eternal change was made as they were born again.
>
> Others had to face up to spiritual crises and many important decisions were made to follow Christ closely, to be useful in His service be it home duties, mission field or full commitment. This latter was part of the leader's experience as well as among the campers.[4]

The 1982 Arura united and ignited fresh energy and focus that blew a tenacious wind into the sails of the Rally movement.

It was an outstanding Arura, with many more to come during the next 33 years.

The 1982 Arura was my first Arura. At the time, I was a leader of the Oamaru Boy's Rally and we managed to encourage a handful of boys and three leaders to attend.

At Aruras, all campers were placed into age-groups, so we were not there as a regional Rally. There were junior, intermediate, senior and young adult boys' and girls' groups. As the boys and girls mixed with their own age groups, they made new friends from around the world.

I was given a tent full of energetic teenage (senior) boys and we had a blast. They were full of life and fortunately I was young enough to keep up with them.

They threw themselves into the whole programme and we all enjoyed the wide variety of activities and sight-seeing trips. My group also had a spiritual hunger and the questions and conversations about God were a daily occurrence.

Each morning I would wake the boys and lead them in a short devotion. This was quality time as the boys were sincerely keen to learn.

Several of those boys went on to become missionaries and one a pastor here in New Zealand. I am still friends with them.

I have attended nine International Rally Aruras over two decades between 1982 and 2004. Each was a unique experience where hundreds of boys and girls from around the world had their lives changed forever.

These Aruras impacted me in many ways. They were all special and contributed to my own development.

Special events like the Aruras have a season to them. Thirty-seven years of Aruras was such a season. They were positive and helpful occasions taking the Rally movement to its highest point.

As times, people and circumstances change, so does the focus.

As Arura numbers dwindled over the years and international travel costs increased, and with declining leader involvement, organising International Aruras became more difficult.

The last Arura in Australia was the Tasmanian Arura in 2012 based at Camp Clayton near Ulverstone. Most of the 240 campers were from Australia and New Zealand. Two were from Northern Ireland.

Northern Ireland hosted its last Arura in 2014 in Bushmills, County Antrim, when over 200 young people enjoyed a week full of activities – including coasteering, deep sea fishing, graffiti workshops, survival courses, beach cleaning, and finishing off with a huge UV party on the last night.

With the guidance of Director Denis Wallace, New Zealand held its last Arura in 2015 at the Christian Youth Camp, Ngāruawāhia. Numbers were small with around 120 campers present. Approximately 10 to 15 Australians made it an international camp.

Since the conclusion of Aruras, gatherings have tended to be localised, national camps for the Rallies within their respective countries.

5

CHANGE

The late Malcolm Barrow, former Rally Leader and Director of Tōtara Springs Christian Centre for many years, once said to me, 'Most movements eventually become a machine, then end up a monument.'

Nothing stays static. Organisations either change or die. To its credit, the EBR and EGR movement has adapted to social and cultural shifts while retaining its primary purpose.

Its first focus has always been to teach the Good News of the Lord Jesus to the minds and hearts of children. The secondary purpose was to grow boys and girls into better young men and women, equipping them for life.

Ask any Rally Leader today and they will admit constant readjusting to the social changes in New Zealand has not been easy.

Some say the 1950s through to the 1970s were wonderful days. There was a greater sense of community and life seemed easier, less stressed and happier.

The 1980s ushered in a generation of big hair, big fashion, liberalisation and excess. The *New Zealand Herald* deemed the 1980s as 'Days of greed and glamour.'

For many it was a time of either amusement or embarrassment. Celebrities were splashed on the television screens and Mum and Dad investors were lured into the share market only to see their investments lost in the October 1987 crash.

In 1956, less than one percent of New Zealanders claimed to have no religious belief. Thirty years later, nearly 18 percent of New Zealanders either said they had no religious belief or did not specify one.[1]

Alarmingly, the marriage rate fell as attitudes to de facto relationships changed. The introduction of 'no-fault divorce' in the Family Proceedings Act 1980 was a major reason the annual divorce rate tripled from five per 1,000 marriages in 1970 to 15 per 1,000 in the early 1980s.[2]

By the late-1980s, the once widely accepted Bible in Schools programme, otherwise known as Religious Education (RE), was in steep decline across the country. Christianity was not as acceptable as it had been for the first seventy years of the 20th century.

In the 1960s almost every Kiwi child was exposed to God, Jesus, the Bible and Christian values through Bible in Schools. Today, less than 5 percent of our precious children have this privilege.[3]

Intolerance, arrogance and political agendas have become common place to remove Christian teachings and influences from society.

It's now apparent many children became unsettled during the 1980s. Society became more secular and with the breakdown of marriages, homes became divided.

Parents shifted into separate homes and their children had to adapt to two different parental environments. Losing the security of a father and mother living under the same roof made many children anxious.

Statistically, in 1951 only a quarter (24.5 percent) of the female labour force were married women. By 1976 this proportion had more than doubled to 56.8 percent. More women were now in the workforce and in the homes where a father and mother were present, both parents were committed to either full or part time work.[4]

Their children became known as 'turnkey' or 'latchkey' kids because they returned to an empty home while their parents worked. As children lacked parental discipline and boundaries, more spoilt children became defiant while others withdrew from social interactions.

Trust was lost in this era, and it made hard work for Rally leaders.

Another factor surfacing in the 80s was the reality many of the existing Rally leaders were aging and struggling to find the energy needed to conduct their Rallies.

The behavioural issues children were displaying were unimaginable compared to the 'good-ol-days' when they first started.

Few younger men and women were interested in Rally work. Young adults faced work and social pressures creating time constraints. The desire to be involved in Rally may have been there, but the stress and strains of managing a family, a career and an income were too great.

This wasn't only a Rally problem. New Zealand society had the same issues with minimal people interested in leading the bowls clubs, the table tennis clubs, the darts clubs and many social groups.

The desire was to be entertained but not be involved in leading. Compounding this attitude was the burgeoning technical revolution. In the early 70s, television was screening local and international programming contributing to children being distracted from a more active and communal lifestyle.

Who could have thought by the turn of the century 'screen time', with television, computers, play-stations and mobile phones, would be a problem in most households?

Changes were also happening in the Open Brethren Assemblies. More churches employed pastors which lessened volunteer input as some believed 'we pay him to do it.'[5]

There is a touch of irony here as Rally endeavours created more work for the local church. A few churches deemed it necessary to employ full-time workers to accommodate the community needs, which in turn was hoped would grow the local church.

For some, the opposite happened. A common attitude was the full-time worker could now do Rally work as part of their church and community responsibilities. Some Rally leaders believed this meant they could withdraw from leading Rally and watch from the sidelines.

The results were mixed. A few churches thrived as they now had someone who could give undivided attention to Rally work as well as their other responsibilities.

Nevertheless, in general Rally work dipped because there were now fewer volunteer leaders. Sadly, evidence suggests many of those early full-time workers and pastors in the Assemblies left their ministry calling because of burnout.[6]

In addition, the Open Brethren churches of New Zealand changed. With so much denominational transfer between churches, there are now people sitting among this network of churches who know nothing of the Rally movement.

Whether they are members, occasional attendees or leaders, many are oblivious of the rich legacy the EBR and EGR have given these churches.

To unite, equip and grow these Open Brethren heritage churches, the majority have gathered under the Christian Community Churches of New Zealand (CCCNZ) umbrella.

This has been a positive and encouraging development as CCCNZ is committed to informing, supporting, building and expanding Gospel opportunities.

As the new Rally movement had people and churches wanting to connect, in the six-years since CCCNZ started seventy-eight churches have linked with this initiative.[7]

With so much changing around them, Rally leaders pressed on as best as they could.

The Rally timeline shown in the table below illustrates a deep commitment among those who have stayed in the movement and who have maintained their drive and enthusiasm.

These faithful servants have given their all and we honour them today because of their example. They truly believed, 'Therefore, since through God's mercy we have this ministry, we do not lose heart' (2 Corinthians 4:1).

Against the tide of society, modernisation and shifting cultural parameters they have kept the vision, walked the talk and been resolute with the mission to reach the boys and girls of New Zealand.

We salute their love and energies given over many years to bring the Gospel to the young people of New Zealand.

There is a reality that we cannot ignore.

The trend of less Rally members and less Rally leaders starting in the late 1980s and continuing through the 1990s, maintained its downward trajectory into the twenty-first century.

Year	Members	Leaders	Rallies
2000	3583	611	145
2002	3015	497	118
2004	2659	465	104
2008	1890	373	72
2011	2083	359	76
2013	1704	340	72
2015	1558	295	67
2018	1230	295	55
2021	1017	230	47

Now, in 2022, it's time to address these declining numbers.

It would be reactionary to say Rally has had its day. It would be unhealthy to think Rally has to stop. We would be fools to ignore the great things achieved over the last 77 years through the Rally movement. King Solomon wisely said to the Princes of Israel, 'Do not move the ancient boundary stone set up by your ancestors' (Proverbs 22:28).

The primary focus of the Rally movement was to bring biblical truth and spiritual awareness to as many boys and girls as possible.

Backed by the Open Brethren heritage churches, for more than 77 years Rally leaders have proclaimed the powerful message, 'God sent His only Son into this world so whoever would believe in Him would not perish but have eternal life' (John 3:16). The result of their blood, sweat, tears and prayers is unmeasurable.

I have mentioned names in this book of people who invested their lives into the EBR and EGR work. These names are listed in the Appendix. In that list alone they have collectively poured over 600 years of their lives in faithfully ministering to the children of New Zealand.

We acknowledge and are grateful for their legacy. In addition, over a thousand other leaders from New Zealand and around the world enabled thousands of children to accept Christ as their Saviour.

Leo Clarke, Les Harris, Robert and Lillian Laidlaw, Nettie Burt and others never moved the Gospel boundary stone when they initiated the EBR and EGR.

They stayed as true as they could and set sail with a new venture that received the fresh wind of the Spirit who enlarged the Gospel boundaries in New Zealand and around the world.

The cornerstone of being Christ-centred and Gospel-focused remained and the Lord blessed and multiplied their efforts with the Rally movement.

Like the men of Issachar (1 Chronicles 12:32), they understood their times and knew what to do. They boldly stepped out in faith and took the Gospel head on into the prevailing culture.

Today, as we contemplate change, we must accept the Gospel is more important than uniforms, more important than hobbies, programmes and camps. They were complementary to presenting the Gospel because at that time they were relevant to the times.

Perhaps they still have a place in attracting young children, but we must not be locked into the mind-set of 'what has worked in the past will work today'.

Some ideas still have their place, but we must also be alert to new initiatives to endorse the Gospel to this generation. We don't need to reinvent the bicycle wheel, but we may need to renew and reshape the rim.

In this twenty-first century, we are facing a new generation of children, adults and social influences. Children and adults seem obsessed with living in the moment to satisfy their needs for pleasure. Selfishness, laziness, apathy and indulgence often appear to be the pursuits of this generation.

Selfies, and self-entitlement, have pervaded character. In the 1950s it was rugby, racing and beer. Today we could identify the average New Zealand attitude as money, me and I don't care.

Some churches have chosen to move away from the Rally model but remain committed to sharing the Bible's message to children.

The Rally movement doesn't have a monopoly on children's ministries. Although these churches once were involved with the Rally work, it's encouraging to see they are using new initiatives to minister to children.

In some cases, they conduct their programmes like Rallies with games, hobbies, character-building exercises, camps and devotions. Instead of calling it a Rally they have a name appropriate to their community.

This is commendable and may the Lord bless their endeavours. Les Harris had this same perspective. He attended a council meeting just before he died where he said, 'Don't change the aims, but we might find a better way to deliver them.'

Like the early Rally leaders who began with the right intent and the right content, we must re-evaluate to see if what has worked in the past will work in the future.

Today, we need thinkers who can explain and grow new ideas, recognise new opportunities and lead with enthusiasm.

They will need to be well grounded in their faith because in today's world they will be confronted.

They will need the support, endorsement and encouragement of their church families who will truly have their backs.

There will be no place for Lone Rangers. The Body of Christ will have to stand by them and with them as a prayerful community of faith.

They will need wisdom with how to best reach into their communities with truth.

They will need to be totally and impeccably trustworthy.

They will need the reinforcement of others whether they are involved directly or indirectly.

They will have to be accountable with their integrity and philanthropy.

They will need assistance with regulatory health and safety requirements.

They will need financial partners to enable them to reach further than ever before.

They need to understand there will be opposition – but God can close the mouths of lions.

They need to have faith that as they honour the Lord, they will see blessings.

They need to be friends of people who will pray and believe light can pierce the darkness with prayers.

They need to understand their Rally history and know the Lord has been among the Rally movement. He has been, He is, and He will continue to honour the Rally efforts if today's leaders 'keep their eyes fixed on Jesus, the author and perfecter of their faith' (Hebrews 12:2).

Above all, today's leaders and all future Rally leaders will need to have an absolute conviction and confidence in the power of the Gospel – 'It is the power of God for the salvation of everyone who believes' (Romans 1:16).

It is the Gospel message every boy and every girl in this land needs to hear. It has always been and always will be a message of hope. In the city and in the country the Bible's message has transformed lives because God's people have diligently lived and spoken it.

As our world and country spirals into self-entitlement, selfishness, materialism, atheistic beliefs and into morbid morality, we cannot remain silent and sit on the side lines.

We are called to be witnesses and no matter where we choose to serve, as a Rally Leader, a deacon, an elder or in any other ministry, we must do the work of an evangelist, 'Preach the Word: be prepared in season and out of season; correct, rebuke and encourage – with great patience and careful instruction' (2 Timothy 4:2).

The EBR and EGR started as an effective movement that saw great blessings. We may now be in a mechanical stage where things are ticking along, but we know we cannot stay there. If we don't change, we are in danger of turning the EBR and EGR into a monument.

What is needed now is a clear, concise, brave look at the future of how EBR and EGR can still be a powerful, life-changing movement.

The thirst for the Gospel message will return even in these secular times, hopefully more strongly than ever, and we must be ready to share it.

6

FUTURE

Imagine the future from a 1944 perspective.

The world is still at war. Suffering continues abroad and at home. Many women are widowed, and thousands of children are being raised fatherless.

Money is short but faith in God remains. Love and hope are the medicine needed for the children who live in New Zealand, so they don't grow up bitter, angry and lost.

On their knees, Leo Clarke, Les Harris, Lillian Laidlaw, Nettie Burt and others seek the Lord's face for guidance, wisdom and courage on what to do and how to do it.

Compelled to help heal the brokenness in young lives, they rise in unity and faith to start the Every Boy's and Every Girl's Rallies. They make mistakes but undeterred, together they press on. They trust God and give their all to this mission.

Before their eyes they see a seed grow and soon the harvest begins. Rallies are launched around the world.

Praise God. But they don't rest on their laurels, and in their enthusiasm, they pass the baton on to new leaders. They gave their utmost for a greater future.

Following those Rally pioneers, in the 70s and 80s a new generation of leaders continued to grow the future and enhance the movement by dreaming bigger and innovating:

- They continued to produce and print Rally magazines
- They initiated the International Aruras
- Guided by Catherine Birch, they produced two editions of the celebrated EBR and EGR Cookbooks. Thousands were printed and many today say the Rally Cookbooks are the best they have ever owned. The proceeds were used to fund the development of the Rally Syllabus
- They produced a four-year Devotional Syllabus created by Helen Martin
- Rally Leader Training Camps were initiated

From 1990 through to 2020:

- Senior National Training Camps were established
- Rally Ambassadors moved and encouraged through the country
- A Rally website was formed
- A Rally Bible was designed, purchased and distributed to Rally members
- A National Rally Facilitator was appointed

The last 77-years reveal a fascinating reflection of courage, resilience and persistence as Rally leaders have continued to grow a programme of hope for the future of every boy and girl they have ministered to.

With steadfast belief, they delivered again and again making our world a better place because of their determination and focus.

Imagine the future from a 2022 perspective.

In 2022 the storm clouds are gathering as more New Zealanders embrace an agnostic worldview.

The aggression against Bible in Schools, the assault on pro-life views, the blitz on euthanasia opponents, the confusing gender agenda, the hijacking of morality and the offense culture that appears to be an increasingly common aspect of today's society, all seems to have numbed and silenced many Christians. Unfortunately, those who are damaged the most from these prolific protagonists are the children of our country.

Our children are the most vulnerable and these cultural shifts are making a fierce attack on the belief structures that have held society secure in the past. Even inside the womb is not safe. In 2019, 12,857 babies were aborted in New Zealand.

Families continue to breakdown at an alarming rate. Children are torn from dysfunctional parents. In our country more than 50 percent of marriages are divorcing, creating uncertainty and despair among children.

Suicide and mental health issues permeate far too many young people. An anti-God agenda is being taught in our public schools. Unnerving identity pressure is forced on our children and teens to accept sexual freedom and transgender ideologies.

Children are under assault from the media, movies and pornography. Self-centredness is destroying their morality, decency and respect for others.

It feels like we are at war. The dark clouds of a global pandemic continue to hover, families are hurting, incomes are tight, fear prevails and many lack hope.

It has the same feel as 1944.

If ever there was a time to have a calculated look at our nation's future, the churches future and our tamariki[1] it is now.

In a sense, 2022 is worse than 1944.

We have global information at our fingertips, but we remain ignorant to truth.

We can communicate around the world in seconds, but we falter in close relationships.

We have more technical advancements to free up our time, yet many are enslaved to screens.

We are more comfortable, but it has made us lazy.

We are healthier than any other generation, but we don't recognise the sickness of sin.

As a nation we have never been richer but morally we are nearly bankrupt.

Belief in God is fading.

Too many churches are losing credibility.

It's time to be on our knees again to seek the Lord's face for guidance, wisdom and courage on what to do and how to do it.

From the powerful example of our past Rally leaders, we know we must rise in unity and step out in faith. 'Without faith it is impossible to please God' (Hebrews 11:6).

The good news message of God's love for a fallen world is still the most profound memorandum for every boy, girl, man and woman on this earth.

We believe this message with all our hearts, and we now must adapt, rethink, redream, and innovate to deliver the message of life to a very different world than 1944.

We won't be able to do this alone. We must stand together, united in purpose and productivity. As Les Harris said in the first edition of the *Rally Leader* magazine:

> It is our earnest wish this Bulletin should be of the greatest possible service to Rally workers. We want to know your problems, and help, if possible, to solve them.
>
> We want to know your desires, and if we can, to meet

them. The whole work is based on mutual co-operation and understanding, and as the Rally movement spreads and grows, we must see to it that this happy spirit is maintained in all that we do.[2]

I suggest the future will need to intentionally develop a Rally operational and programme renaissance.

We will have to embrace technology. Let's face it, many children are technologically smarter than us and know their way around their devices better than adults do. We also know the technology growing their minds can destroy their minds.

In a digital age, Rally leaders will have to upskill and have equipment available to attract children who love their devices. Teaching online safety and warning of traps on the internet are essential factors for our children today.

One Rally during the 2020 Covid-19 lockdown conducted online Rally programmes. During that time, they gained new online members. I'm in awe of their competence and initiative.

The New Zealand Education system has failed many children. I know of high school teachers who lament that when young teens arrive for their secondary learning, far too many can't read, write or do maths adequately.

This is a gap that Rallies could help with. Teaching the positives of healthy, elementary learning skills will encourage parents to send their children to Rally. I believe there is already a pilot after-school programming with this intent. This is marvellous.

Although our health professionals recognise obesity is a growing issue and more children have become couch potatoes with a sedentary lifestyle, I believe most Kiwi kids love sports.

The reason isn't the sport itself; it's the social interaction they enjoy. Rallies could have an early skillset programme teaching the basics of catch and throw, running and jumping, teaching coordination and respect for others. This is not in competition to community sporting teams, but rather a partnership of introducing children to physical activities to grow their confidence and respect for others – 'kids in sports stay out of courts.'

Our morality and value system must be above reproach. Far too many institutions and organisations have failed their children. Sexual, emotional and physical abuse has dogged the church and many homes now distrust any organisation wanting to take their children away.

By God's grace the Rally movement has retained its good name. I know there have been cases of abuse, but in most cases, they have been dealt with justly and correctly. Brand 'Rally' is still trusted and many past members loved and valued their Rally days. Now, as parents, they need to be assured their children will be safe every time they go to Rally.

We need to have a Code of Conduct and an accountability system to raise the bar for all faith-based organisations.

The goal is to protect our young and to provide an environment where every parent and every child can trust their Rally leaders.

The 1943 census estimated there were 269,775 children aged between 5 and 14 in New Zealand.

New Zealand's Children's Commissioner states, 'There are 1.2 million children under the age of 18 in New Zealand – that's about a quarter of the country's population.'[3]

What a harvest field lies before us. This country is fertile with considerably more children than in 1944. These are children who need to know God loves them, and that genuine Rally leaders care for them and their families.

Additionally, increased community migration has brought ethnic diversity to the children in our cities and towns. These are people, families and children who long to be accepted and are trying to assimilate into their new environment.

Helping them comprehend our language, culture and communities is a door the Rallies could move through. When we offer to accept, honour and accommodate their children we win their appreciation.

With a greater mission field and more children before us, it is no longer tenable to rely solely on donated time for this national and international movement.

It has been an astute move to appoint Tony Foster as the New Zealand Rally Facilitator. Tony's appointment is a collaborative move between the Christian Community Churches of New Zealand (CCCNZ), the National Rally Council and Rutland Street Church, Christchurch.

Tony is the great, great grandson of Captain Robert Neville who was saved at a 'Sailors' Rest' meeting while on shore leave in Port Chalmers, Dunedin, in 1875.

As a captain of ships of the Union Steamship Company, he was well respected and became a capable preacher at the Sailors' Rest in many ports.[4]

The Every Man's Hut outreach grew out of the Sailors' Rest work and The Every Boy's Rally movement began on the back of the Every Man's Hut ministry.

It's a positive thing to see the generational links here. Tony's affirming input into various Rallies nationwide has lifted the enthusiasm for this strategic work. He is ably supported by his wife Angela, who now has an administrative role with the Rally Trust.

We need more of the right people to take the Rally movement to the next level. We must invest in this remarkable outreach mission like never before. 'The harvest is plentiful, but the workers are few' (Matthew 9:37).

As churches we need to fan new, invigorated leaders into flame. We must support them at every level. We entrust the Gospel to them and consequently must stand with them, providing for their practical needs so they remain empowered with the mission.

If we appreciate the fact that the Rally movement has been the greatest and most effective youth undertaking in the history of the Open Brethren heritage churches, we must continue to use the medium of Rally to reach New Zealand's children.

As a modern movement we need to adapt, but not just for community awareness. We need to let all past Rally members, who are now parents, know Rally still exists, still works, is still investing healthy truths into young hearts and can still be trusted.

I was encouraged by the report in the August 2021 edition of the *Rally Leader* magazine, which indicates that the points above are being addressed.

With confidence, the National Rally Council have changed their name to the New Zealand Every Boy's and Girl's Rally Trust. Their new slogan is 'Preparing Kids For Life'. As a Trust they have established a Governance Board to grow the Rally Team. They will enhance the vision and mission of Rally by overseeing the finances, policies and direction of the Rally movement.

They are committed to 'facilitating and encouraging inter-Rally communication and events, create resources, manage finances, report on activities, oversee prayer-teams and administer the Rally website'.

The Rally Trust says, 'Our heart to see more children encountering Christ through Rally has motivated this.'

This new phase deserves praise and endorsement. The gatekeepers of this movement understand and value the heritage of what has been achieved. Clearly, they have taken up the baton of faith and are adapting to the cultural challenges before them. I salute their resolve and decisive determination to honour the continuation of the Gospel to the young people of New Zealand.

As churches we must uphold and reinforce the Rally Trust and every Rally Leader in the country. They must not feel alone in their endeavours.

The future will reveal if 'Cometh the hour cometh the church.'

The 75th Rally Anniversary was celebrated at Willow Park Christian Convention Centre, Auckland, in June 2019.

Guest speaker Russell Burt, who in 2021 was awarded the New Zealand Order of Merit (MNZM), gave a stirring message to all guests in attendance. He reminded us that every child in New Zealand needs to be welcomed and loved, just as the Lord Jesus welcomed and loved children. He brought our attention to the transformative message that Jesus Christ wants to enter and change every young life.

Pointing out the obvious, he said there was no shortage of children here in this great country. The problem is that the Rally programme has a shortage of volunteer leaders committed to the vision, purpose and belief of the Gospel.

In his closing comments he urged for a national prayer campaign to ask the Lord of the harvest for new Gospel-focused Rally leaders here in Aotearoa. He said, 'Bible in Schools may be taken from us, but they can't take Rally off us, or our Sunday schools, or our youth groups, or our camps.' His message was profound and prophetic.

For 78 years, the New Zealand Rally movement has been a light in the darkness. For almost eight decades, faithful men and women have tirelessly reached into their communities to bring hope, joy, peace and balance to the confusion.

Their examples and unheralded witness have helped change many hearts, homes and communities for the better. Without their sincere involvement up and down this land and patient service, New Zealand would be more godless than it is.

Founding leaders Leo Clarke, Les Harris and others believed that despite the prevailing winds against them, it was their duty, their joy, to advance a cause that would help individual hearts and heal a society.

They had their struggles. It was no easy thing to grow a small hobby group into a world-wide movement, but the Lord honoured their commitment and blessed the EBR and EGR vision in a significant and unforgettable way.

Before those good men and women and the leaders who worked with them died, Rallies had been established in almost every corner of the world. Every week, thousands of children heard the good news of Jesus Christ.

Multitudes were saved and have contributed to a better society. Many were added to a plethora of church families and went on to marry, establish Christian homes and raise confident children.

Some became missionaries, church and community leaders.

The evidence suggests the forefathers of the Rally movement understood that 'nothing changes if nothing changes'. Together, the EBR and EGR leaders confronted the culture of the day and rather than being influenced by it, they decided to change it.

Like the great cloud of witnesses in Hebrews 12:1, their examples echo down through the years and their voices are speaking to us today. They ask us to be on our knees as we seek to save the lost. They ask us to work together to reach every community in New Zealand.

They want us to understand their hopes were realised as they entrusted every effort to their Lord. They left us with a powerful reminder the impossible can be done if the Lord is with us. They gave us a legacy and an indication of just how good the future can be. They believed Jesus showed the way when He said, 'Let the children come' (Matthew 19:14).

We know our Lord loved and treasured the faith of every child. The Apostle John confirmed this when he wrote, 'To all who received Him, to those who believed in His name, He gave the right to become children of God' (John 1:12).

New Zealand was a different place in 1944. The nation was anxious, hurting and struggling financially. Domestically, many children were fatherless and single mothers needed encouragement. As our Kiwi soldiers were fighting the final battles in Europe, the Second World War in the Pacific was nearing its horrific climax. Hope was needed.

In my assessment, New Zealand in 2022 is a spiritually darker place. The battle for the minds and hearts of our young people has landed on our shores. Morals have plummeted.

Media driven, social and political agendas are godless, and faith is fading. Conspiracy theories fill the air. Misinformation is everywhere fed by thoughtless and provocative tweets, blogs and posts.

As a nation, we appear to be on a shameless, depraved and unethical downward spiral. We must refuse to be caught up with rumours and the secular rhetoric relentlessly seducing our energies and priorities.

More than ever, truth, hope, character and God's love remain the church's mandate to our society, especially to our children.

It's time to stand up and reinforce our Rallies.

They have proven to be a God-blessed youth movement. The foundation stone the first Rally leaders placed remains a firm reminder of what the Lord will bless. Their mission was about the Gospel. Our mission is about the Gospel.

The Gospel compels us on into the storm, to win some. As we build upon the groundwork of previous leaders, it is now our responsibility to endorse and lead a new generation of children to Christ.

As in 1944, it will take our united support to urgently and confidently proclaim the Gospel up and down this great land. If we rise in obedience, in our lifetime, we will see even greater things yet to come.

Will you rally with us to be part of tomorrow's future, and serve in the mighty mission before us?

AFTERWORD

By Tony Foster & Mark Grace

I have been blessed to witness God at work through the NZ Rally movement.

Beginning in 2019, it has been my privilege to meet past and present leaders, church leaders and children across Aotearoa.

I acknowledge the many leaders who have and continue to serve our God wholeheartedly. The Lord has blessed their efforts and many people have come to faith as a result.

The New Zealand Rallies are now entering a season of transition. We're seeing things happening that give us hope as we move into the future. With increasing interest in regional camps, CCCNZ encouragement, recent financial support, new Rallies starting and this book of NZ Rally history, I believe Rally will be a major contributor to reaching the nation for Christ.

We acknowledge the challenges ahead. Families are time-stressed, many struggle financially, are spiritually poor and are unaware of God's love for them. God has the blueprint for their lives and the NZ Rally Trust is committed to supporting, guiding and encouraging these families spiritually, educationally and physically.

We aim to resource and equip leaders in new ways, to grow the next generation to love the Lord their God with all their heart and to love their neighbours. Meeting these goals, the council recognises the need to appoint people who can strengthen and facilitate, administrate, communicate and help with curriculum development. We have funding from generous supporters to enable us to establish these roles.

Developing the www.nzrally.org.nz website gave us the opportunity to upload Bible lessons, health and safety documents, supportive practical guides and points of interest for Rally members and leaders. We're also progressing with a social media presence. These formats will keep leaders informed in real-time with new ideas to reinforce their valuable work. Increasing the Rally prayer team is another initiative to engage and endorse the Rally advancement.

God will have future trade personnel, doctors, nurses, accountants, lawyers, schoolteachers, bosses and maybe even a Prime Minister in our midst. Through our investments in them as children, how good would it be if they were God-fearing, well-equipped citizens God raised through the NZ Rally movement?

If you would like to be part of this, please contact us and we will include you in our prayer team.

God Defend New Zealand.

Tony Foster
NZ Rally Facilitator

What you've just read is an awesome story of God working through ordinary Christians, in ordinary churches over many decades to point young people across the country to Christ through the Rally movement.

This was done with a deep commitment to gospel content and creative communication. In the Rally movement you didn't need to choose between content and creativity.

This was done with a commitment to treating children and youth as whole people developing their character, their wisdom, helping them physically and developing them into flourishing members of churches and communities

New Zealand is changing rapidly. Rally itself is in a quiet season of transition to meet these changes. We are resourcing Rally leaders with new online material. We'll be communicating as much digitally as in print. We are working on new regional camps and starting new Rallies across the country.

We'll be making it easier for parents to find a Rally and to bring their children to it. We've appointed staff to serve and support local churches and their amazing Rally leaders. These are all under the hood, behind the scenes changes.

What isn't changing is our commitment to point children and youth to Jesus Christ, through the gospel from the scriptures through a local church Rally.

What isn't changing is our commitment to gospel clarity and creative communication, ministering to children and youth as whole people, spiritually, physically and emotionally.

What isn't changing is our reliance on God and seeking his leading and provision for the work of Rally locally, regionally and nationally.

If you're a current Rally Leader we are grateful to God for you. We are looking forward to serving you and the amazing work you and your church do through Rally.

If you've been a Rally volunteer in the past, thank you, we would love you to consider receiving our news updates. Please partner with us and pray for Rally.

Mark Grace
Chairman, Rally Trust

ROLL CALL

More than a thousand men and women have served with distinction for Every Boy's and Every Girl's Rallies in New Zealand.

Many are no longer with us but their legacy lives on. Some are still serving and their commitment to this ministry inspires us today.

My omission of many important names is regrettable. It doesn't mean their contributions are forgotten. We respect every person who has contributed to Every Boy's Rally (EBR) and Every Girl's Rally (EGR) work.

I confined my research to the early developmental years, the key people involved, and included a few of those in the movement today.

Ashby, Graham   Rally Leader Oamaru, Rally Ambassador 1995-2006.

Barrow, Malcolm   Rally Leader Auckland and Waikato, Director Tōtara Springs Christian Centre Matamata, 1970 to 1990, Director 1982, 1990 New Zealand Aruras.

Birch, Catherine Rally Leader Feilding, married Bill and served more than 60 years in Wellington specialising in craft and woodwork. Catherine collated, edited and tested every recipe in the well-received *Rally Cookbook 1*, 1979 and *Rally Cookbook 2*, 1987. She served on Rally Council for 10 years.

Birch, William (Bill) Rally Leader Christchurch and Upper Hutt, involved for 60 years.

Burt, Nettie Co-founder of EGR in Auckland in 1945.

Burt, Russell Worked with Rallies in Auckland, now Principal of Point England School where he runs an afterschool programme modelled on the Rally aims.

Clarke, Bruce Nephew of Leo Clarke, attended Epsom and Takapuna Boy's Rallies, became a Cadet at North Bridge EBR. As a young adult travelled to many Rallies and camps showing films. Rally Leader in Matamata and member of the Waikato Rally Executive, Rally Council eight years.

Clarke, Leo Founder of EBR 1944, Auckland. Rally Council member for 16 years.

Coppin, Jim First Secretary 1961 Rally Council served 16 years. Based in Whakatāne, son of renowned evangelist Enoch Coppin.

Finn, Jim

1940s, Ran boys' clubs and camps at Akatarawa, Tararua Ranges. When the EBR formed in 1944, Jim was the first to establish Rallies in Wellington starting Moera EBR at the Gospel Hall, Randwick Road. Boys were taken from the age of 10 and numbers were high. Jim's enthusiasm supported more Rallies in the region.

Foster, Tony

Rally Leader Rutland Street Church, Christchurch, New Zealand National Rally Facilitator since 2019.

Foster, Angela

Rally Leader Rutland Street Church, Christchurch, New Zealand National Rally Administrator since 2021.

Gauntlett, M.C.G.

Chairman inaugural 1946 Waikato/Bay of Plenty District Committee.

Grace, Mark

Chairman New Zealand Boys' and Girls' Rally Trust since 2020. Mark serves as Christian Community Churches of New Zealand (CCCNZ) Ambassador.

Grant, Cecil

Friend of Leo Clarke, co-founded Rallies in Wellington and Hutt Valley. Civil Servant (non-uniformed) New Zealand Navy. Head of Naval Stores, Wellington. New Zealand Diplomat to England, purchasing battleships. Chairman of the Board for Gospel Publishing House.

Cecil's wife Phyllis helped start the first Every Girl's Rally in Wellington.

Grindlay, Diane   Rally Leader, Auckland and Dunedin, Rally Council member 1998-2019 serving 21 years.

Harris, Les   Co-founder of the EBR in 1944, Auckland. Rally Council member for 18 years.

Hughes, Isa   Secretary on the inaugural 1946 Waikato/Bay of Plenty District Committee for 14 years.

Jackson, Bob   Initial Rally Council member where he acted as secretary for 23 years between 1968 and 1991. When Bob retired from teaching, he began regular visits around Auckland to encourage Rallies. He served in the movement for at least 40 years.

Jeffers, Fred   Before EBR the Jeffers had large groups of boys at their dining table doing various woodwork hobbies. They moved to a local hall in Ellerslie with 120 boys each week. Fred joined Harris and Clarke to make the badge and motto book of this club which they decided to call 'Every Boy's Rally'.

Jeffers, Margaret   Margaret supported Rally endeavours, and the later work of a large Bible study youth group. She also led the Girl's Rally in Wellington for some years and taught Bible in Schools.

Laidlaw, Robert   Founder of Farmer's Trading Company, Rally financial supporter.

Laidlaw, Lillian   Co-founder of the EGR in Auckland 1945.

Lind, Mavis   Rally Leader in Feilding, Bulls and Mangakino with husband Tom.

Lind, Norman (Norm)   Rally Leader in Feilding, major contributor to training Rally leaders throughout New Zealand. Norm had many years on planning committees for Aruras and Senior National Camps and 25 years on the National Council, Chairman for eight years, retiring in 2006. Norm retired from Rally involvement after 54 years.

Lind, Shirley   Rally Leader in Feilding serving beside husband Norm. She gave 50 years of service to Girl's Rally work.

Lind, Thomas (Tom)   Rally Leader in Feilding, Bulls and Mangakino, 1956 established Lake Whakamaru Campsite, developed Waikato and Bay of Plenty Boy's Rallies Residential Cadet Leadership Course. This developed into a national coeducational programme.

Marsh, Les   Known as 'Skipper', 1951, first editor Rally

Leaders and Members magazines. Rally Council nine years. In 1972 Les and his wife travelled to 40 countries visiting missionaries. Les based his outstanding book *In His Name* describing the work Open Brethren missionaries were doing around the world. Commended by the Feilding Assembly to Papua New Guinea in 1974.

Melhop, Alan   Rally Leader Invercargill 50 years, founder Lakeland Park Christian Camp, Queenstown. Rally Council member and Chairman 25 years.

Melhop, Harold   Rally Leader Invercargill 50 years, Chairman of first Rally Council established in 1961, with his brother Alan co-founded Lakeland Park Christian Camp, Queenstown.

McClunie, Dale   Rally Leader Te Awamutu, Rally Council member from 1994. Editor Rally Members magazine since 1996. Active in Rally work for 50 years.

McConnell, Betty   Rally Leader Auckland, Editor EGR magazines and Girl's badge manuals, Rally Council member 25 years. Awarded Queen's Service Medal 1992 for distinctive service to youth work.

McCracken, Jack Chief Mechanic for Leo Clarke. Supported and grew EBR and EGR movement.

Swallow, Frederick Auckland Rallies. Editor Every Boy's Rally Leaders Bulletin.

Turner, Ruth Current Rally Supplies provider. Contact: nzrallysupplies@gmail.com.

Wallace, Denis Saved as a boy through the Rally work, Leader Manawaru EBR. Rally Council 1991 served 29 years, 14 years Chairman. Director 2010, 2015 Rally Arura.

Wallace, Joy Leader Manawaru EGR, continues with combined EBR and EGR.

ENDNOTES

Chapter 1 – History
1. www3.stats.govt.nz/New_Zealand_Official_Yearbooks/1945/ NZOYB_1945.html#idsect2_1_32302
2. en.wikipedia.org/wiki/Bill_Pratney
3. www.kennett.co.nz/product/bill-pratney
4. Ngaire Avenue Gospel Hall later changed its name to Ngaire Avenue Bible Chapel.
5. The Open Brethren churches were a collective of churches who did not like to be identified as a denomination. They preferred an autonomous connection where each church building had its own name, but collectively they were called 'Assemblies'. Each individual church was known as an Assembly.
6. Les Marsh, *In His Name*, pp.64, 125-126.
7. nzhistory.govt.nz/culture/the-1920s/overview
8. nzhistory.govt.nz/war/western-front-1917
9. Obituary notice, *Treasury Magazine*, November 1984.
10. Ibid, p.3.
11. Taken from ibid.
12. The Rally Motto adopted in 1944 was taken from 1 Peter 2:17 (KJV) but was later changed to Ecclesiastes 12:1. 'Remember your Creator in the days of your youth.' This reflected a more understandable and acceptable explanation to the purpose of Rally.

Chapter 2 – Hope
1. Peter J. Lineham, *There We Found Brethren*, p.127.
2. Ibid., p.160.
3. www.ralliesni.com/pages/about-rallies-ni/history-of-the-rallies

Chapter 3 – Growth

1. Crescent Church, Belfast, Woodford, Bethany (Finaghy) Belfast, Scrabo (Newtownards) and Silverbirch (Bangor). Source: Mrs Ann Hamill & Glen Johnson, 2021.
2. Feilding's input into the Rally movement nationally is clearly seen in: Thomas Lind, Lake Whakamaru Camp; Les Marsh, first Rally Editor; Catherine Birch, Council member and cookbook editor; Norm Lind, Council member, Training Director, Chairman; Grace Print, Rally Supplies and Council member; Mark Grace, current Rally Trust chairman.
3. *The Rally Standard*, March-April 1962. Vol. 1, No. 1.
4. Ibid.
5. Catherine Birch, *50 Years of Rally in the Wellington District*.
6. en.wikipedia.org/wiki/Paul_Reeves
7. As calculated on the Reserve Bank Inflation Calculator. www.inflationtool.com/new-zealand-dollar/1967-to-present-value?amount=50
8. Information gathered for this chapter was given by Robert Park (Palmerston North), Rally articles supplied by Catherine Birch (Upper Hutt), Dale McClunie (Te Awamutu), Diane Grindlay (Dunedin) and material the author has gathered.

Chapter 4 – Aruras

1. Tony Collis, *One Million Children*, Life Communications, 2019, p.23.
2. *Rally Leaders Bulletin*, 1982 Vol. 32, No. 1.
3. As described in R. A Storey, *Matamata History & 50th Jubilee*.
4. *Rally Leaders Bulletin*, 1982 Vol. 32, No. 1.

Chapter 5 – Change

1. nzhistory.govt.nz/culture/the-1980s/overview
2. Ibid.
3. Tony Collis, *One Million Children*, Life Communications, 2019, p.20.
4. Craig Ashby, *Principles in Practice: A Historical Analysis of the Trend towards Employing Pastors in the Open Brethren Churches of New Zealand*, 2013, p.45
5. Ibid., pp.38-42.
6. gbjournal.org/8-82/
7. www.cccnz.nz/linked-in-churches/

Chapter 6 – Future

1. Māori word for 'children'.
2. *Every Boy's & Every Girl's Rally Bulletin for Leaders*, issued quarterly or as required, April 1951 (No.1), edited by L. A. Marsh, 490 Parnell Road, Auckland, C.4, N.Z.
3. www.occ.org.nz/our-work/statsonkids/#:~:text=Statistics%20 and%20information%20on%20the,quarter%20of%20the%20 country's%20population
4. Peter J. Lineham, *There We Found Brethren*, p.110.

ABOUT THE AUTHOR

Graham Ashby was a rebellious lad who grew up in a stressed and dysfunctional home. In his autobiography *An Unexpected Life* he recounts the positive impact Rally leaders and the wider Rally movement had on his life, shaping his heart and his future. From a Rally boy, Cadet and Group Leader he developed into a Rally Leader and served as the first New Zealand Rally Ambassador between 1995 and 2006.

Graham has spoken at numerous Rallies in New Zealand, Australia and in Northern Ireland and attended nine international Aruras. In his 50-year association with the Every Boy's and Every Girl's Rally movement, he has brought the same life-changing message that changed him to thousands of Rally members and leaders around the world.

These experiences mean that Graham is in a unique position to look back and look forward; to reflect and offer insights to the investment this ministry makes to the children of New Zealand and beyond.

For 36 years Graham has worked full-time as a travelling minister primarily among the Open Brethren heritage churches, now known as Christian Community Churches of New Zealand (CCCNZ), and other evangelical denominations. Graham is married to Wanda. They have two married adult children and three grandchildren.